the amazing sacrament

A celebration of the Eucharist

by Stephen Redmond SJ

First published 2005 by
Veritas Publications
7/8 Lower Abbey Street
Dublin 1
Ireland
Email publications@veritas.ie
Website www.veritas.ie

ISBN 1 85390 887 8

A catalogue record for this book
is available from the British Library.

Printed in the Republic of Ireland
by Betaprint Ltd.

Veritas books are printed on paper made from the wood pulp
of managed forests. For every tree felled, at least one tree is
planted, thereby renewing natural resources.

In this gift (of the Eucharist) Jesus Christ entrusted to his Church the perennial making present of the paschal event (the Last Supper and what followed it), bringing about a mysterious 'oneness in time' between that event and the course of the centuries.

The thought of this evokes profound amazement and gratitude... This amazement should always fill the Church assembled to celebrate the Eucharist... I would like to rekindle this Eucharistic amazement.

John Paul II: *Ecclesia de Eucharistia*
(Church from Eucharist)

In grateful tribute to all my living and departed
friends in the Eucharist

Contents

eUCHaRISt: HIStORy

I remember seeing many years ago in the museum of Mount Melleray Abbey a set of dummy books. The 'books' were entitled *De Nimia Caritate Dei* (*Concerning the Boundless Love of God*). It was a penal-day tabernacle. A reminder of the fidelity of our ancestors to the faith in times of persecution. A reminder too that the Eucharist is a unique outpouring of God's love for us.

The Church has been a part of human history for two millennia and has experienced many changes. But the basics, the elements in the Church that flow directly from its ultimate source, the Blessed Trinity, remain unchanged; and one of these, the centre and heart of the life of the Church, is the Eucharist.

From East to West

It has been in the world since that Thursday evening, as we would call it, when 'the Lord Jesus on the night when he was betrayed took bread and when he had given thanks, he broke it and said, This is my body which is for you. Do this in remembrance of me. In the same way also he took the cup, after supper, saying, This cup is the new covenant in my blood. Do this, as often as you drink it, in remembrance of me.'

This is Saint Paul's account of its institution in his first letter to the Christians of Corinth, written about thirty years after the first Holy Thursday with the Eucharist already a living reality in the Church. It is the earliest account we have, antedating those in Matthew 26, Mark 14 and Luke 22.

We get sightings of the Eucharist in the very early Church: for instance, Justin's outline of Mass as celebrated in Rome about 150, substantially identical with our rite, and Hippolytus' text from about 200, which we now use almost word for word as the second Eucharistic Prayer. Later the Eucharistic event was inset into elaborate liturgies in various parts of the Church. The Latin Roman rite became predominant in the West. In our own time the Roman liturgy has been revised with, among other things, a swing to vernaculars and a re-emphasis on the role of the laity.

The Eucharist has been celebrated in many cultures and languages during those two millennia. The first of those languages must have been Aramaic, the vernacular of the Lord and the apostles and their first converts, but with the spread of the Church beyond Palestine, Greek, then an international language, became dominant in Christian worship and the re-present-ing memorial of the Last Supper got a Greek name: *Eucharistia*. From, say, the fourth century Latin began to replace Greek in the West. Eastern Christians, whether Catholic or not, kept their tradition of celebrating in various languages. Since the Second Vatican Council Mass in the Roman rite is nearly always celebrated in the vernacular with Latin holding a primacy of doctrine and honour.

'The Altar of the World'
On the first Holy Thursday the Lord told his disciples Peter and John to go to a certain house and say to the man of the house: "'The Teacher says, where is the guest room where I

am to eat the passover with my disciples?" And he will show you a large upper room furnished'. (Luke 22, 11-12)

There have been so many 'upper rooms': the houses of the first Christians; the sanctuaries of early Christian Ireland and Britain; basilicas, cathedrals, parish and monastic churches; 'safe houses' in Tudor England and Mass-rocks in penal-day Ireland; the trenches of war and the hermitages of peace; makeshift shelters like the Ark of Kilbaha in Clare and wide open-air spaces like the Phoenix Park in Dublin. I remember a friend of mine flopping down on the grass in the ruined church at Bodenstown in County Kildare and saying, 'I like to pray wherever Mass was said'. As Pope John Paul says lyrically in *Ecclesia de Eucharistia* (echoing Teilhard de Chardin), 'the Eucharist is always in some way celebrated on the altar of the world'.

And, we can add with Saint Paul, the Eucharist will remain until the end of the world as we know it: 'As often as you eat this bread and drink the cup, you proclaim the death of the Lord until he comes' (1 Corinthians 11,26): an element of Christ's tremendous parting promise: 'I will be with you always, to the close of the age' (Matthew 28, 20). He is still Emmanuel: God with us.

> Ruins: the grass is high
> here Christ arrived, passed by
> here the Mass was said
>
> The church across the way
> here Christ comes every day
> here the Mass is said
>
> Until that secret hour
> when Christ returns in power
> the Mass will still be said

Chapter two

eucharist: essence

Enfolded and clothed, as it were, in so many variables of culture, language, time and place are three related core facts about the Eucharist: Christ becoming present, Christ sacrificing and being sacrificed, Christ nourishing.

Presence
The glorious risen Christ in his totality becomes present. By the power of God through the ministry of the priest who acts in the person of Christ, the substance, the inner basic reality of bread and wine (what makes bread to be bread and wine to be wine in ordinary estimation), is changed into the substance of the body and blood of Christ. But he becomes present as he is: so blood, soul and divinity are present too under the appearances of bread and body, soul and divinity are present too under the appearances of wine, and of course, body, blood and soul are constituents of a glorified humanity.

'In the most blessed sacrament of the Eucharist, the body and blood together with the soul and divinity of our Lord Jesus Christ, and therefore the whole Christ is truly, really and substantially contained' (Council of Trent). 'This presence... is presence in the fullest sense... substantial presence, by which Christ, God and one of us, makes himself wholly and entirely present' (Paul VI: *The Mystery of Faith*).

To believe in this presence is one of the greatest of Christian graces: a grace for the mind and will ('senses fail and faith alone assures the mind that Christ has come' – *Pange Lingua*): meant to be the prelude to an eternal experiencing of the risen Lord in both divinity and humanity.

Priest and Sacrifice

Christ becomes present as a sacrifice. 'The making of this sacrament (the Eucharist) is a sacrifice', says Saint Thomas Aquinas. And Christ is its priest. Last Supper, Calvary and Mass are one sacrifice in the sense that Priest and Gift and Love are one and the same in all three. Only the mode of offering is different: the Cross involves actual blood-shedding, actual death; the Supper and Mass do not. In the Mass the risen Christ continually 're-presents' himself in a way suitable to his pilgrim people (the Lover adapting to his beloved), inviting them to unite themselves with him in self-giving.

Echoing the Council of Trent and indeed the traditional faith of the Church in *Ecclesia de Eucharistia*, Pope John Paul says that Christ gave the Church the Eucharist as the perennial making-present of the paschal event (Last Supper, Passion and Death, Resurrection), thus bringing about a 'oneness in time' between that event and history. The thought of this, he says, evokes 'profound amazement and gratitude'. The ideal Mass congregation and officiating priest are a community lost in wonder and thanks.

Nourishment

Christ nourishes. In Communion he keeps his stupendous gospel promises: 'He who eats my flesh and drinks my blood

has eternal life and I will raise him up on the last day. He...
remains in me and I in him. As the living Father sent me, and
I live because of the Father, so he who eats me will live
because of me' (John 6:54, 56, 57). The words are stark and
urgent. They shocked many of their first hearers. They are
words of love.

The beautiful antiphon of the solemnity of the Body and
Blood of Christ (Corpus Christi) echoes the doctrine and
promises in John: 'O holy banquet, in which Christ is received,
the memorial of his Passion is celebrated, mind and heart are
filled with grace and a pledge of future glory is given to us'.

Christ as our high-priest is the chief minister of all the
sacraments. He is of course a most loving minister. According
to Saint Thomas Aquinas (endorsed by, among others, Pope
John Paul) all the other sacraments are oriented towards,
converge on, the Eucharist. The other sacraments come from
Christ. The Eucharist is Christ. In a uniquely concentrated
way it is the sacrament of his love for us. He associates that
love for us with the love-gift of himself to his heavenly Father
in Passion and Death and Eucharist.

Love evokes love. Our best response to his love (a
response in complete keeping with the specific purpose of
this sacrament) is a practical Eucharist-centred gospel-
minded love of God and others: with God's help to 'walk in
love, as Christ loved us and gave himself up for us, a fragrant
offering and sacrifice to God' (Ephesians 5, 2). So we
proclaim and pray:

> For all there is one Christ
> for all one loving Lord is sacrificed
> one living Bread we eat
> to bind and hold us close and firm
> as God's own blessed wheat

And may this Eucharist-Gift
arise and shine across the world's dark drift
that all may see and come
and find in Him their All-Desired
and in his love be one

We praise you, Trinity
the Father, Son and Spirit, Blessed Three
we thank You and adore
and share in Eucharist the pledge
of life forevermore.

Chapter three

teaching and testimony

Saint Paul (1st century)

The persecutor of the very early Church who experienced the most famous conversion in Christian history. A giant figure of the New Testament (of which his epistles, unique in religious literature, form a large part), proclaiming Christ as crucified and risen Lord.

The cup of blessing which we bless, is it not a communion in the blood of Christ? The bread which we bless, is it not a communion in the body of Christ? Because there is one bread, we who are many are one body, for we all partake of the one bread (1 Corinthians 10, 16-17).

For I received from the Lord what I also passed on to you, that the Lord Jesus on the night when he was betrayed took bread, and when he had given thanks, he broke it and said, 'this is my body which is for you. Do this in remembrance of me'. In the same way also the cup, after supper, saying 'this cup is the new covenant in my blood. Do this, as often as you drink it, in remembrance of me'. For as often as you eat this bread and drink the cup, you proclaim the death of the Lord until he comes (1 Corinthians 11, 23-26)

Saint Ignatius of Antioch (2nd century)

The Christian community in Antioch, the splendid capital of Syria, was founded in apostolic times. Ignatius was one of its first bishops. The text given here is from one of the letters he wrote to various communities while on his way to martyrdom in Rome.

Be careful to take part in one Eucharist for there is one flesh of our Lord Jesus Christ and one cup for his one blood, one altar, as there is one bishop with his presbyterium...

The heretics abstain from Eucharist and prayer because they do not believe that the Eucharist is the flesh of our Saviour Jesus Christ who suffered for our sins and whom the Father in his great kindness raised.

You come together, breaking the one bread that provides the medicine of immortality, the antidote against death, the food of life forever in Jesus Christ.

Saint Justin (2nd century)

A layman and philosopher convert from paganism, Justin exercised an intellectual apostolate aimed at educated pagans: exemplified here by his account of the Mass as he knew it. He died a martyr – ironically in the reign of the philosopher emperor Marcus Aurelius. A good patron saint for lay Christians engaged in intellectual pursuits – preferably apostolic!

Bread and a cup of watered wine are brought to him who presides over the brothers. Accepting these he praises and glorifies the Father of all through the name of his Son and the Holy Spirit and gives thanks at length for these gifts. When he has prayed and given thanks, all the people shout 'Amen'. 'Amen' in Hebrew means 'so be it'. After the thanksgiving of the president and the acclamation of the people, those we call deacons distribute the bread and watered wine over which thanks has been given to those present and bring them to those absent.

We call this food 'Eucharist'. No one is allowed to partake of it unless he believes our teaching, has been washed as to forgiveness of sins and re-birth and lives in keeping with what Christ taught. The food that nourishes our own flesh and blood by being changed and over which thanks has been given through a prayer containing his words is the flesh and blood of that incarnate Jesus.

For the apostles in their commentaries which we call gospels have related that Jesus so commanded them: that, having accepted the bread and given thanks, he said, 'Do this in remembrance of me, this is my body': that in the same way, having accepted the cup and given thanks, he said, 'this is my blood'...

Saint Irenaeus (2nd century)
Bishop of Lyons and one of the most important teachers in the early Church. He emphasised the goodness of material things, Christ as the

redeeming, engracing, unifying Lord of creation and the historical continuity of the Church with Christ and the apostles. He presented the Eucharist as the pledge of bodily resurrection. A good patron saint for environmentalists!

> He (Christ) taught the new offering of the New Covenant which the Church receives from the apostles and offers to God through all the world... The way we think is in tune with the Eucharist and the Eucharist ratifies the way we think.

Saint Cyril of Jerusalem (4th century)

Bishop of Jerusalem and famous for his baptismal instructions: perhaps the greatest catechist of the early Church.

> In the sign of bread the body is given to you and in the sign of wine the blood, so that by partaking of the body and blood of Christ you may be 'con-bodied' and 'con-blooded' with him: we become Christ-bearers.

Saint John Chrysostom (4th century)

'John of the Golden Mouth (Chrysostomos)', priest of Antioch and patriarch of the imperial city Constantinople where his uncompromising eloquence made enemies in high places. His stormy career ended in exile and virtual martyrdom. Commonly referred to as 'Doctor of the Eucharist'. Much venerated in the Orthodox Church.

> It is not we who cause the offerings to become the body and blood of Christ, but Christ himself who was crucified for us. The priest... speaks these words but the power and grace are

of God. 'This is my body', he says. This statement transforms the offerings... He who did this at the Supper is the same who acts now. We rank as ministers: it is he who consecrates and changes.

Saint Augustine (4th–5th century)

Baptised in his thirties after years of philosophical searching and (according to himself but he may well be exaggerating his sinfulness) sexual excess. Bishop of Hippo Regius in modern Algeria. Best-known Father of the Church, 'Doctor of Grace', the chief theological influence in the western Church for centuries. Voluminous writer: most famous books The City of God *and* The Confessions, *the latter being the most renowned autobiography in Christian history.*

The assembly and society of the saints is to be offered to God by that high priest who offered himself for us... This is the Christian sacrifice: 'we, the many, are one body in Christ' (Romans 12,5). The Church celebrates this in the sacrament of the altar, so well known to believers, in which it is clear that in that offering the Church is offered.

The body of Christ can live only by the spirit of Christ. O sacrament of piety! O sign of unity! O bond of charity! He who desires to live has where to live and by what to live.

He who suffered for us entrusted to us in this sacrament his own body and blood and this he makes us: we have become his body and through his mercy we are that which we receive.

Saint Thomas Aquinas (13th century)
A glory of the Dominicans and a 'great' in the history of philosophy and theology. Immensely influential in the Council of Trent.

Insofar as it is a memorial of the Lord's Passion which was a true sacrifice, this sacrament is called a sacrifice. As a sign of Church unity it is called a communion: it unites us with Christ, we share in his humanity and divinity, we are united to one another. Insofar as this sacrament prefigures our fulfilment in God in heaven, it is called provision for the journey because it supplies the wherewithal to get us there. And in this respect it is also called Eucharist, that is, beautiful Gift, for that is what Christ is.

The presence of the true body and blood of Christ in this sacrament cannot be discovered by sense or intellect, but only by faith which is based on divine authority... This presence is in keeping with the perfection of the New Law. The sacrifice of the Old Law contained the true sacrifice of Christ's Passion only figuratively. The sacrifice of the New Law instituted by Christ needed to have something more: that it should contain not only in sign and figure, but in very truth the Christ who suffered. And so the sacrament which really contains Christ perfects all the other sacraments in which the power of Christ is shared.

This presence is in harmony with the love of Christ whereby for our salvation he took to himself a true body of our nature. Friends love to live together, so he promises us his bodily presence as a reward... Meanwhile on our pilgrimage he does not deprive us of his bodily presence but joins us to himself in this sacrament through the reality of his body and blood. And so this sacrament, because of such a close union of Christ with us, is a sign of supreme love and an uplifting of our hope.

This conversion or change (of the substance of bread and wine into the substance of the body and blood of Christ) is not like natural changes but is entirely supernatural, brought about only by divine power... God is infinite act... and so God's action extends to the entire nature of being. God is able not only to bring about formal change (that is, the succession of different forms in the same subject) but also the change of the whole being – that is, the change of the whole substance of one thing into the whole substance of another. And this is done by divine power in this sacrament.

Saint Catherine of Siena (14th century)
Siena's most famous citizen. Mystic, member of Dominican Third Order, 'mother' of a 'family' seeking spiritual guidance, adviser to two Popes at a time of Church crisis, offering her life for a Church gravely wounded by schism. The text given here is from her Dialogue written shortly before her death.

My providence has given (my people) nourishment to renew their strength in the course of their pilgrimage in this life... What is that nourishment? It is the Body and Blood of Christ crucified, true God and truly human, the bread of angels, the bread of life.

In receiving this sacrament the soul remains in Me and I remain in the soul. As the fish is in the sea and the sea is in the fish, so I am in the soul and the soul is in Me, the Ocean of peace.

The Council of Trent (16th century)

This council was convoked to introduce some badly needed reforms in the Church and to re-state Catholic doctrine in response to the Protestant challenge.

Our Saviour instituted this sacrament when he was about to leave this world and go to the Father. In it, as it were, he poured out the riches of his love for us... and commanded us to celebrate in receiving it a memorial of himself and to announce his death until he came to judge the world. He wanted this sacrament to be received as the spiritual food of souls, as the nourishment and strength of those alive with the life of him who said, 'he who eats me will live because of me', and as the remedy by which we are freed from daily faults and preserved from mortal sins. Moreover he wanted it to be the pledge of our future glory and eternal happiness and the symbol of that one body of which he is the head. He wanted us to be very closely bound as members of that body in faith, hope and love...

The holy synod openly and simply professes that in the life-giving sacrament of the Eucharist after the consecration of the bread and wine our Lord Jesus Christ, true God and truly one of us, is truly, really and substantially contained under the appearance of those natural things.

This faith has always been in the Church of God: that immediately after the consecration the true body of our Lord and his true blood exist under the appearance of bread and wine along with his soul and divinity.

This holy Council declares: by the consecration there comes about a conversion of the whole substance of bread into the substance of the body of Christ our Lord and of the whole substance of wine into the substance of his blood.

He (Jesus Christ), our God and Lord, was to offer himself once on the altar of the cross in death – to God the Father to achieve eternal redemption. But his priesthood was not to be ended by death; and so at the last supper on the night he was betrayed, he left his Church a visible sacrifice (such as human nature demands). By that sacrifice the sacrifice with blood-shedding that was to be enacted once on the Cross was to be re-presented, the memorialising of it was to last to the end of the world and its saving power was to be brought to bear on the forgiving of our daily sins.

He offered his body and blood under the appearance of bread and wine to God the Father. He gave his body and blood under those same signs to his apostles to receive and by the words 'do this in memory of me' he ordained them priests of the New Covenant and commanded them and their successors in the priesthood to offer as well.

In this divine sacrifice which is done in the Mass that same Christ is contained in a sacrifice without the shedding of his blood who on the altar of the Cross once offered himself with the shedding of his blood... There is one and the same victim, now offering through the ministry of the priesthood, who then offered himself on the cross. The only difference is the mode of offering.

The holy synod urges, asks and implores that all of the Christian name... should believe in and venerate these sacred mysteries of Christ's Body and Blood with that constant and firm faith, devotion of mind, piety and worship with which they can frequently receive that supersubstantial bread; so that it may truly be for them the life of the soul and the perpetual health of the mind: by its strengthening vigour they can, after their trying pilgrim journey, reach their heavenly homeland to experience that same bread of angels completely unhidden which they now experience only under sacred veils.

Venerable John Henry Newman (19th century.)

Newman was a leading member of the Oxford Movement which advocated a Catholicising interpretation of Anglican doctrine. He became a Catholic in 1845 and later an Oratorian and cardinal. In the 1850s he was rector of the Catholic University in Dublin. The excerpt given here is from his novel Loss and Gain. *He was noted for saying Mass both raptly and rapidly.*

The Mass is a great action, the greatest action that can be on earth. It is not the invocation merely, but if I dare use the word, the evocation of the Eternal. He becomes present on the altar in flesh and blood, before whom angels bow and devils tremble. This is that awful event which is the end, and is the interpretation, of every part of the solemnity. Words are necessary, but as means, not as ends; they are not mere addresses to the throne of grace, they are instruments of what is far higher, of consecration, of sacrifice.

They hurry on as if impatient to fulfil their mission. Quickly they go, the whole is quick; for they are all parts of one integral action. Quickly they go; for they are awful words of sacrifice, they are a work too great to delay upon; as when it was said in the beginning, 'what thou doest, do quickly'. Quickly they pass; for the Lord Jesus goes with them, as He passed along the lake in the days of his flesh, quickly calling first one, then another. Quickly they pass; because as the lightning which shineth from one part of the heavens into the other, so is the coming of the Son of Man. Quickly they pass; for they are as the words of Moses... And as Moses on the mountain so we too 'make haste and bow our heads to the earth and adore'.

Pope Saint Pius X (20th century)
This decree was issued by command of the Pope. Its background was theological debate concerning the dispositions required for frequent and daily communion with some moralists taking a very strict stance. The decree forbade any such future debate. In a later decree Pius authorised communion for young children who could distinguish between the sacramental species and ordinary bread.

Frequent and daily communion is to be accessible to all the faithful of Christ of whatever class or circumstances, so that no one who approaches the holy table in the state of grace and with a right and religious attitude can be prevented from so doing.

A right attitude means this: that the person approaching the holy table should not do so for the sake of (mere) use or out of vanity or for human reasons but should wish to do what pleases God, to be united more closely in love with God and to avail of that divine medicine for his/her weaknesses and defects.

It is very desirable that those availing of frequent and daily communion should be free from at least fully deliberate venial sins and a disposition towards them. Nevertheless it suffices that they be free from mortal sins and have the resolve of never sinning in future... Care is to be had that there be a diligent preparation for holy communion and a suitable thanksgiving afterwards.

Willie Doyle (20th century)

A member of the Irish Jesuit province. As a young priest he felt called to a life of great penance, consuming zeal, virtually continuous prayer. He became a legend of courage and devotedness as a chaplain in World War I. He died by shell-hit at Frezenberg, Belgium in August 1917. This text is from a letter of his.

By cutting a piece out of the side of the trench I was just able to stand in front of my tiny altar, a biscuit box supported on two German bayonets...

Round about me on every side was the biggest congregation I ever had: behind the altar, on either side, and in front, row after row, sometimes crowding one upon the other, but all quiet and silent, as if they were straining their ears to catch every syllable of that tremendous act of Sacrifice – but every man was dead!

Some had lain there for a week and were foul and horrible to look at, with faces black and green. Others had only just fallen, and seemed rather sleeping than dead, but they lay, for none had time to bury them, brave fellows, every one, friend and foe alike, while I held in my unworthy hands the God of Battles, their Creator and their Judge, and prayed Him to give rest to their souls. Surely that Mass for the Dead, in the midst of and surrounded by the dead, was an experience not easily to be forgotten.

Stephen Redmond SJ (20th century)

My father and I were together at the final Mass of the Eucharistic Congress in Dublin in 1932. It was a feast of sight and sound: the Fifteen Acres in the Phoenix Park turned into a vast church with a congregation of a million; the white expanse of the domed altar-space and flanking colonnades; the voice of Pope Pius XI from Rome; John McCormack singing *Panis Angelicus*; at the consecration the clunk of Saint Patrick's Bell spanning fifteen centuries of the Eucharist in Ireland and the soldiers' sunlit swords held high in homage.

Rohiyah ('Spirit of Light') was a convert from Islam. The Sacred Heart sister who had prepared her told me that every time she came to the convent for instruction she visited the Blessed Sacrament. Just after I baptised her she suddenly disappeared. 'She's in the chapel', sister said. And there we found her, deep in prayer, intent on One.

Saint Edith (Teresa Benedicta) Stein (20th century)

The German Jewish intellectual who became a Catholic and a Carmelite. A victim of the horrific Nazi 'Final Solution' in Auschwitz in August 1942. The text given here is from her 'The Prayer of the Church'.

Jesus was a religiously practising Jew. He took part in the Jewish liturgy and by pronouncing the age-old ritual promises he invested them with new life. It was indeed when he transformed the Passover bread and wine into his Body and Blood that the life of the Church began.

The Second Vatican Council (20th century)

The main objectives of this Council, convoked by Pope John XXIII, were to present the Catholic faith in contemporary terms, in a way that would enhance the faith-life of Catholics and increase the Church in the world, and to promote Christian unity.

In regard to the Eucharist, the Council restated the traditional teaching on the essentials: Christ present, Christ sacrificing and being sacrificed, Christ nourishing. Echoing Saint Thomas Aquinas, it held that the other sacraments cohere with and converge towards the Eucharist. In the Eucharist the Church finds all its good: Christ himself. In the Eucharist the covenant between God and humanity is renewed.

The Council highlighted the link between the laity and the Eucharist. By baptism the laity share in the priesthood of Christ: a true priesthood though essentially different from that conferred in Holy Orders. Their chief priestly act is to take part in the offering of the Eucharist. This sacrament is a very special source of grace and holiness and praise of God, of that love which is the heart of the lay apostolate. It is in fact the source and summit of all evangelisation. All that the laity do 'in the Spirit', all that they patiently endure, are sacrifices to be offered with Christ in the Eucharist. By their Christian commitment in so many places, the laity consecrate the world to God.

The council in effect says that the baptised laity are called to be important ministers in the renewal of the covenant between God and humanity, in the Mass on the altar of the world.

Chapter Four

Church from Eucharist:
Highlights

This encyclical is a personalised document. Pope John Paul is clearly speaking from his heart on a Reality which matters enormously to him. He mentions experiences of the Eucharist which helped to shape his life. Here and there the tone is passionate. We could almost call the encyclical a love-letter, filled with 'a profound amazement and gratitude' for this one Gift given through the centuries.

Priest, Sacrifice, Banquet

He states the traditional doctrine of the Church about the Eucharist: that in the Mass there is a sacrifice in which Christ is priest and sacrificial Gift and which sacramentally makes the essence of the sacrifice on Calvary present again; that under the appearance of bread and wine Christ is uniquely present and is the spiritual nourishment of those who receive him.

He insists that the Mass is far more than a 'fraternal meal'; that it is centred on a sacrifice which sacramentally makes the Cross present in our ongoing lives. In a very strong passage on dignity in the celebration of the Eucharist he says that 'the Church has never trivialised the intimacy of a banquet with her Spouse by forgetting that he is also her Lord. The banquet that Christ truly is is 'a sacrificial banquet marked by the blood shed on Golgotha'.

Call to Love

He emphasises that the Eucharist, the action of the Church on earth, expresses and strengthens our union with the blessed in heaven. He also makes the important related point that the Eucharist reminds us of our responsibility to those who share the planet with us, especially those who are at risk, in need. (Here he mentions the need to work for justice and peace and defend the right to life from conception to natural death, and a 'globalisation' that threatens the poorest and weakest). He reminds us of the feet-washing serving Christ at the last Supper (John 13) and of what Saint Paul thought of those who combined the Eucharist with dissension and indifference towards the poor (1 Corinthians 11). Echoing the Second Vatican Council (and, we may add, the handbook of the Legion of Mary), he calls the Eucharist 'the source and summit of all evangelisation', of all apostolic outreach.

Resurrection, Adoration, Unity

He points out that the Resurrection was part of the paschal event and that it is the risen Lord who is in the Eucharist. He encourages both pastors and people to pray to and adore the Blessed Sacrament outside of Mass: a practice full of grace, deriving from the Eucharistic sacrifice and directed towards Communion both sacramental and spiritual.

The Eucharist is the sacrament of the unity of the Church both as regards visible and invisible bonds of union. Sunday Mass is especially important for this unity. As long as such unity is incomplete, full concelebration of the

Eucharist with those of Christian traditions not in full communion with the Catholic Church is not possible. But in special circumstances Holy Communion can be given to individuals of such traditions.

Woman of the Eucharist

Pope John Paul is well known for his devotion to Our Lady. Not surprisingly a remarkable and indeed lyrical chapter of the encyclical is given to her as 'Woman of the Eucharist'.

He sees her as a role model for ourselves in our attitude to this greatest of the sacraments. There is a 'profound analogy' between her 'Fiat, Yes' at the Annunciation and our 'Amen' at the moment of Holy Communion (and perhaps we could add, at the end of the Eucharistic Prayer). Her daily life was a kind of 'spiritual communion', of 'anticipated Eucharist', a pattern of sacrifice that culminated in the Passion and Death. He envisages for her a sharing in the Eucharist that was a uniquely intimate welcoming of Christ and a re-living of her experience at the Cross.

On Calvary the Lord gave her to us, as represented by the beloved disciple, to be our spiritual Mother. Our celebration of the sacramental memorial of the Cross involves our accepting her as precisely that and allowing her to accompany us.

He asks us to re-read Mary's great song the *Magnificat* in a 'Eucharistic key'. The Eucharist is primarily praise and thanksgiving. So is the *Magnificat*. We have been given the Eucharist so that this song may express our life as it expresses hers.

Praise and Hope

The conclusion of the encyclical is a kind of song of praise of 'the amazing sacrament': a treasure, the heart of the world, the pledge of human fulfilment, vigilantly guarded, not to be exploited or devalued, but to 'be experienced and lived in its integrity'. 'In the Eucharist Christ walks beside us... and enables us to become, for everyone, witnesses of hope'. That hope-filled sentence, echoing Emmaus (Luke 24), is specially relevant to believers in the Eucharist at the present time.

Chapter five

Prayers of the Mass

Prayer before Mass
Lord, visit and purify our consciences, so that when Jesus Christ your Son our Lord comes, he may find in us a dwelling prepared for him.

Prayers from the Liturgy of the Eucharist
These bread and wine prayers at the Preparation of the Gifts, introduced into the Mass after Vatican Two, are based on models from the 'Mishnah (Repetition)', the book of rabbinic instruction. They are an ecumenical reminder of the Jewish source of much of our worship.

> Blessed are you, Lord, God of the universe.
> Of your great goodness we have received this bread/this wine which we offer you; fruit of the earth/fruit of the vine and of our hands. It will become for us the bread of life/spiritual drink.

The mingling of water and wine in the Eucharist goes back, it seems certain, to the Last Supper itself. The prayer we use in the Roman Mass is very ancient. It was originally a Christmas prayer in the Ambrosian liturgy in Milan.

By the mystery of this water and wine may we become sharers of the divinity of him who humbled himself to become a sharer of our humanity.

The *Veni, Sanctificator* was a Celtic contribution to the pre-Eucharistic Prayer sequence of the Roman rite which predominated in the Western Church. The Vatican Two liturgical revisers found it inappropriate, but ensured that the Holy Spirit was invoked (not directly, but through the Father) in newly-authorised Eucharistic Prayers. Perhaps we could use it as a formula of dedication for places, projects and people (including ourselves) in praise of the Person who is the mutual Love of the Father and the Son.

Come, Sanctifier, almighty and eternal God:
bless this sacrifice prepared to your holy name.

The 'Holy, Holy, Holy' from Isaiah's temple experience (Isaiah 6) is another example of Jewish liturgical influence. It came into the Roman Mass at an early date and was soon joined by the Palm Sunday acclamation of Jesus as given in Matthew 21 and Mark 11. The Aramaic 'Hosanna' means 'Save, we pray' but it was also used as something like our 'Hurrah'. The 'Holy-Hosanna' need not be confined to the Mass: it can be seen as an 'environment' prayer of praise and thanks. With the 'Blessed is he...' it forms a hymn of praise and welcome to the Christ who is soon to be sacramentally present:

Holy, holy, holy Lord, all-powerful God
heaven and earth are filled with your glory

Hosanna in the highest
Blessed is he who comes in the name of the Lord
Hosanna in the highest.

The beautiful prayer for peace is partly derived from the Lord's discourse after the Last Supper (John 14, 17). The 'Lamb of God' prayer recalls John the Baptist's acknowledgement of Jesus as Saviour (John 1, 29). It came as a plea for mercy into the Roman Mass in the seventh century. At first it accompanied the breaking of the species of bread. When 'hosts' came into use the sequence was shortened and was ended with a plea for peace. The Vatican Two liturgy envisages a partial return to the original practice. Before Communion the priest says one of two prayers. These prayers and the prayer for peace have been in the Roman Mass for a millennium.

> Lord Jesus Christ: you said to your apostles: I leave you peace, I give you my peace. Do not look upon our sins but on the faith of your Church and grant it peace and unity according to your will.

> Lamb of God you take away the sins of the world: have mercy on us. Lamb of God, you take away the sins of the world: have mercy on us. Lamb of God, you take away the sins of the world: grant us peace.

> Lord Jesus Christ, Son of the living God: by the will of the Father and the co-working of the Holy Spirit, through your death you have given life to the world. By your most holy Body and Blood free me from all my sins and from every evil, make me always hold fast to your commandments and never let me be parted from you.

> Lord Jesus Christ: do not let the receiving of your Body and Blood bring a judgement and condemnation against me but may it protect and heal me in mind and body.

The invitation to receive Communion echoes and reflects the spectacular and visionary scene in Revelation (19: 6-9) of the mystical eternal marriage between Christ the risen Lamb and the redeemed and radiant Church: a reminder of the glory that our Communion here and now is meant to lead to.

The centurion of Capernaum (a centurion was the equivalent, more or less, of the modern non-commissioned officer) has been in the Mass for many centuries in both Eastern and Western liturgies. Let us pray for others at this point in the Mass: after all, the good decent man whose words we use was asking for someone else (Matthew 8, Luke 7):

> This is the Lamb of God who takes away the sins of the world. Blessed are those who are called to the Supper of the Lamb.

> Lord, I am not worthy that you should enter under my roof. Only say the word and my soul shall be healed.

CHAPTER SIX

Prayers of Lovers of the Eucharist

Saint Augustine

> O sacrament of reverential love! O sign of unity!
> O bond of charity!

Saint Fulgentius of Ruspe (an adaptation of part of a treatise)

> Spirit, you filled his Heart with love
> so he was sacrificed
> now bread and wine await your touch
> to change them into Christ
>
> Transform us, Spirit, touch us too
> to follow him who died
> to learn that all who rise like him
> must first be crucified.

Saint Thomas Aquinas

> Almighty and eternal God: I approach the
> sacrament of your only-begotten Son, Our Lord
> Jesus Christ. I approach as one sick to the

physician of life, as one soiled to the fountain of mercy, as one blind to the light of eternal radiance, as one poor and needy to the Lord of heaven and earth.

I beg from the abundance of your generosity: heal my sickness, wash away my dirt, enlighten my blindness, enrich my poverty, clothe my nakedness: so that I may receive the Bread of angels, the King of kings and Lord of lords, with the reverence and humility, the sorrow and devotion, the purity and faith, the purpose and intention that will advance the salvation of my soul.

May I receive not only the sacrament of the Lord's Body and Blood but also its full truth and power. May I so receive that Body which was his from the Virgin Mary that I may deserve to be integrated in his mystical body and numbered among his members.

Most loving Father: now on my pilgrim way I intend to receive your beloved Son sacramentally veiled. Grant that I may finally contemplate him unveiled forevermore.

Saint Bonaventure

Most dear Lord Jesus: transfix my very depths with the utterly sweet and health-giving wound of your true, serene, apostolic and most holy love... Grant that I may hunger for you, the bread of angels... whom angels desire to see... May I always thirst for you, the fountain of life, wisdom, knowledge, eternal light, torrent of delight and richness of the house of God... May I always seek you and find you... doing everything to the praise and glory of your name humbly, wisely, lovingly, delightedly... with perseverance to the end so that you alone may be my hope... my delight... my peace...

The Author of *The Imitation of Christ*

Rejoice, my soul, and give thanks to God for so generous a gift and so unique a consolation left to you in this valley of tears. For as often as you celebrate this mystery and receive the body of Christ you attend to the work of your redemption... When you celebrate or hear Mass, it should be as great, as new, as joyful to you as if on this day Christ had come for the first time into the Virgin's womb being made one of us or suffered and died on the Cross for our salvation... You have prepared a great supper... your most sacred body and blood... you rejoice all believers with a holy banquet, you enrapture them with the cup of salvation in which are all the delights of paradise... O grace beyond words! O thoughtfulness to be wondered at! O immense love uniquely lavished on us!

Soul of Christ (attributed to Pope John XXII)
(Strictly a Passion prayer but very suitable for Communion. Sung as 'Soul of my Saviour'. A favourite prayer of Saint Ignatius Loyola and John Henry Newman)

Soul of Christ, sanctify me. Body of Christ, save me. Blood of Christ, put me in ecstasy. Water from the side of Christ, wash me. Passion of Christ, strengthen me. O good Jesus, hear me. In your wounds hide and shelter me. Never let me be parted, Lord, from thee. From the foe defend me. In death's hour call me. Bid me come, bid me come to thee where I may praise thee, Lord, eternally.

Venerable John Henry Newman

Such a sacrifice (Calvary) was not to be forgotten. It was not to be – it could not be – a mere event in the world's history... to pass away except in its obscure unrecognised effects. If that great deed was what we believe it to be, what we know it is, it must remain present, though past; it must be a standing fact for all times... Yes, my Lord, though Thou hast left the world, Thou are daily offered up in the Mass... Thou remainest a Priest forever.

My Lord, I offer Thee myself in turn as a sacrifice of thanksgiving. Thou hast died for me and I in turn make myself over to Thee. I am not my own. Thou has bought me; I will by my own act and deed complete the purchase... My praise and strength shall be in Thee. Enable me to carry out what I profess.

prayers of Lovers of the eucharist

Saint Thérèse (a paraphrase of one of her poems)

Let me be the key that opens wide your door
let me be the light announcing you are here
let me be the flame, a message from your Heart
a text of love, a signal strong and clear.

Make me altar-stone and make me altar-cloth
(Mother in a cave, a Baby rocked to rest)
let me shine in gold: a monstrance, paten, cup
and there you'd be my loving Lord and Guest

Blessed chosen wheat that grew in God's own fields
blessed chosen grapes matured by God's own sun
now they're bread and wine awaiting words of love
transform me, Lord, with them and make us one.

Venerable Charles de Foucauld

In the blessed Eucharist You are whole and entire, all-loving, my beloved Jesus, as fully as You were in the house of the Holy Family of Nazareth, in the house of Magdalen at Bethany, as You were in the midst of your apostles. In the same way You are here, my Beloved and my All. And grant this grace, my God, not only to me but to all your children, in You, through You, for You. Give us our daily bread, give to all that true bread which is the sacred host. Grant that all may love, venerate, adore It and may glorify You and console your Heart throughout the world. Amen.

Venerable Edel Quinn (An adaptation of retreat notes)

O Blessed Trinity: I unite myself with Christ in his Sacrifice of himself in this Mass. I do this to your glory, in thanksgiving for everything and for your people, especially for those who cannot come to Mass because of sickness, distance, work or war. I place this intention in Mary's hands.

Jesus, let me be more in your company in the Blessed Sacrament, with you in your own adoring of your Father. Mother Mary, pray and adore for me.

CHAPTER SEVEN

PRAYERS OF THE
IRISH TRADITION

These prayers express a profound faith and a tradition to be treasured.

Fore-Prayers (*Reamh-Guíeanna*)

Blessed Sunday! Welcome, praise!
crown of all the seven days
day and night for meeting Christ
for keeping tryst

Dé do bheatha chugainn, a Dhomhnaigh beannaithe
a thagainn chugainn i gceann na seachtainne
lá agus oíche chun Críost a fhreagairt.

We walk in blessed company:
Mary on her way with friends
to join her Son on Calvary
to share a Love that never ends

Siúlaimid mar aon leis an Mhaighdean Muire
agus leis na daoine eile
a bhí ag tionlacan a hAonMhic ar Chnoc Chalvaire.

Welcome, King of Sunday, Mary's son
Risen Lord of Easter – victory won!

Céad fáilte romhat, a Rí an Domhnaigh ghlórmhair, a
Mhic na hÓighe is a Rí a rinne an t-aiséirí.

I offer my mind with the mind of the Mass
my thoughts, desires and heart
through the prayers of Our Lady this blessing I
ask
a Christian's share and part

Ofráilim m'intinn le hintinn an Aifrinn
mo chroí, mo smaointe agus m'aigne
trí impí na Bantiarna beannaithe
cion Críostaí a thabhairt dom den Aifreann

Consecration *(An Coisreacan)*

A hundred thousand welcomes, blessed Body
the Body that was crucified and slain
welcome, only Son of God, our Saviour
welcome, Lord, again, again, again

Céad míle fáilte romhat, a Cholainn bheannaithe
céad míle fáilte romhat, a Choirp a céasadh
céad míle fáilte roimh do Chorp, a Thiarna
a AonMhic De, 's é do Bheatha.

A hundred thousand welcomes, King of Sunday!
Céad míle fáilte romhat, a Rí an Domhnaigh!

Communion *(An Chomaoineach)*
Redeeming Father like the ocean sun
forgive us all the sins we've ever done
from heaven, Father, say the healing word
that joyfully we may receive the Lord

A Athair ghil a cheannaigh sinn
agus atá mar ghrian ar muir
go maithe tú gach peaca dúinn
a rinnearmar riamh 'gus inniu
ar neamh go maithe tú, a Dhia, ár gcoir
gur taitneamhach go nglacaimid ár dTiarna inniu.

I give myself to you, dear Lord, today
never, ever, Jesus, let us part
at hour of death, don't let me slip away
and after death enfold me in your Heart

Toirbhirm duitse mé féin, a Chríost
nár scara mé leat a choích 'arís
ar uair mo bháis ná lig dom imeacht
's i ndiaidh mo bháis bím leat i bhfolacht.

I have you now: Lord, stay forevermore
dear heaven on earth, give healing, make me whole
Jesus, my deepest love and faithful friend
protect me now and on that final shore
I say this now lest words should fail my soul
when senses fail and Eucharist will end

Tá tú agam anois, go bhfanair agam go brách
Ó a Neamh ar talamh, maith agus mórshláinte
go ndéana tú do m'anam
'Íosa mhilis, a dhianghrá
coimirce m'anam ar do dheasláimh anois agus ar uair mo
bháis
ar eagla, an uair dheireanach, nach dtiocfadh liom é 'rá

I welcome you in love and courtesy
my welcome's like a torrent full and free
like a father's for his infant in the womb
Stay, Lord – in my heart there's always room.

Fáilte mharthanach mhúinte chóir romhat, a Thiarna
fáilte mar an taoile tuile romhat
fáilte an athar roimh an leanbh atá i mbroinn go fóill romhat
fanacht gan imeacht ach fanach linn féin go deo romhat

A hundred thousand welcomes to you, dear
sweet Lord
I love you, Mary's Son
give unworthy me a corner in your house
just a little one

A Thiarna mhilis, céad míle fáilte
a Mhic Mhuire, gráim thú
Cé hé mise ar chóir dom teacht chugat?
A Rí neimhe, déan cúinne beag dom.

Thanks for the Mass *(Buíochas ar son an Aifrinn)*
We praise you, God of majesty
for giving us, your family,
This holy Mass, this legacy
that we might live sin-free

Sármholadh duit, a Dhia mhóir
ar son an Aifrinn Naofa chóir
a d'fhág tú ag do daoine bocht'
lena gcoinneáil saor ó pheaca is locht.

Hymnal of the Eucharist

List of Songs

The word-texts and melodies of these hymns are by Stephen Redmond SJ except where another derivation is given. 'African' means that he first heard the melody in Zambia.

Bring Your Bread and Wine

change them, make them all div-ine his re-al-i-

ty. Come and make a start

All you are, will ev-er be All your life and

lib-er-ty Bring them to his Heart

Bring them to his Heart.

CONSECRATING WORD

African

Here is bread___ here is wine___ these we of-fer as a sign___ of our liv-ing of our giv-ing Je - sus, we pray: Say your liv-ing con-sec-rat - ing word change our off-'rings in-to you, O Lord. Just a Lord.

Just a simple presentation
something taken from creation
things of eating, things of greeting
Jesus, we pray: say your living consecrating word
and we'll offer and receive you, Lord

Bread and wine – here's the start
of the showing of his Heart
he will take them and remake them
Jesus, we pray: say your living consecrating word
and we'll share your death and life, O Lord

Let me be the Key

(paraphrase of a poem by Saint Thérèse of Lisieux)

Make me altar-stone and make me altar-cloth
(Mother in a cave, a Baby rocked to rest)
let me shine in gold: a monstrance, paten, cup
and there you'd be my loving Lord and Guest

Blessed chosen wheat that grew in God's own fields
blessed chosen grapes matured by God's own sun
now they're bread and wine awaiting words of love
transform me, Lord, with them and make us one.

Sow the Wheat

Moderate tempo

Sow the wheat make it bread to eat

plant the vine make it in - to wine

you're the Lord all cre - a - tion's in your

hand, in your hand. Here is bread,

make it Christ in - stead Here is wine

make it all div - ine you're the Lord

do the won-der that you've planned, that you've

BReaD aND WINe

Bread and wine won't last forever
Very soon the power that's his
will enfold them like a river
change them into all he is

Bread and wine from his creation:
hands and earth and rain and sun
Now they're signs of his salvation
to become the Holy One.

Bread and wine – he left this token:
grains that bind and drops that blend
Blood that flowed, a Body broken:
One who loved us to the end.

Bread and wine – a sign of others
Bread and wine – that's where we start
Make us truly sisters, brothers
Jesus, open wide our heart.

HOLY!

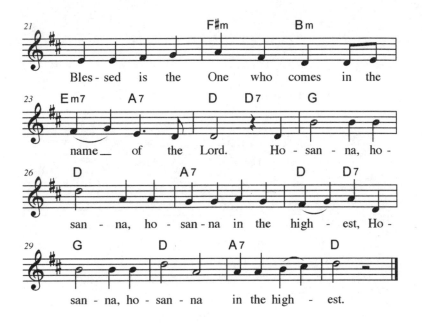

Bles - sed is the One who comes in the name _ of the Lord. Ho - san - na, ho - san - na, ho - san - na in the high - est, Ho - san - na, ho - san - na in the high - est.

acclamation

Rather slowly

C   G7   C   G7   C   C7

Christ has died,   Christ is ri - sen,

Dm   Gsus4 G7   C   G7

Christ will come a - gain.   Christ has died,

C G7 C C7   Dm   G7   C

Christ is ri - sen,   Christ will come a - gain.

Dm   Gsus4 G7   Dm   Gsus4 G7

Al - le - lu - ia   Al - le - lu - ia

C   G7   C   G C C7   Dm   G7   C

Christ has died, Christ is ri-sen, Christ will come a - gain.

Great amen

Rather slowly

A - men   A - - men___

Al - le - lu - ia   A - men   A - men__

Al - le - lu - ia.

a Song to Celebrate
(Pange Lingua)

Make a song to ce - le - brate this
Eu - cha - ris - tic mys - te - ry
glo - rious Bo - dy, pre - cious Blood, the
ran - som paid to set us free
Ma - ry's Son, the Lord of na - tions,
Heart of God's own li - tur-gy. A - men.

Given to us and born for us of Mary ever-virginal
Giving us the gospel word to know the Father, hear his call
ending life as priest and gift in one momentous festival

Supper-room and friends together, paschal moon, his final night
Exodus: the great tradition, legal forms and ancient rite
then he gives himself as food: an act of love, an act of might.

Word-made-flesh makes bread his flesh: with just a word the deed is done
then the cup: the wine becomes the precious Blood of Mary's son
senses fail and faith alone assures the mind that Christ has come

Let us therefore venerate this greatest of the sacraments
patterns of the past foretold this crowning act of providence
let our faith enrich our mind, discover all that's veiled to sense.

To the Father, to the Son incarnate in this mystery
praise and glory, power, thanksgiving as it was, is now, shall be
to their Love, the Holy Spirit, equal praise eternally. Amen.

The Latin text can be sung to this melody.

Pange Lingua, Verbum Supernum *and* O Sacrum Convivium *are from the* Office of Corpus et Sanguis Christi *and are traditionally ascribed to Saint Thomas Aquinas. But it seems clear that he was the compiler of the Office rather than its author. The* Adoro Te *is also credited to him. The last two stanzas of the* Pange *and* Verbum *became the standard hymns for Benediction of the Blessed Sacrament.*

Heavenly Word
(Verbum Supernum)

Moderate tempo

You are the heav'n - ly Word with
Fa - ther end - less - ly your life that sets us
free comes near its end.
You give your-self, dear Lord, as food of ran - som
paid while you are being be - trayed by so - called
friend. A - men.

Quickly the deed is done:
beneath a twofold sign
both human and divine the living Lord

One of us, Mary's Son
the One the Father sent
companion, nourishment, the price, reward

War with the enemy:
come, save, be at our side
dear Gift that opens wide the heavenly door

Praise to the One, the Three
the Lord who loves to give
who brings us home to live eternally. Amen.

Holy Banquet
(O Sacrum Convivium)

Ho - ly ban - quet, hea - ven-sent

Christ him - self our nour - ish-ment me -

mor - ial of his Pas-sion, of his death on Cal - va -

ry.___ Gift to fill the heart with grace

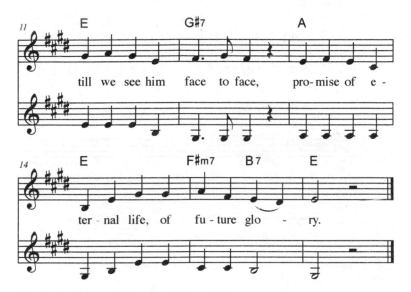

The Latin text can be sung to this melody.

Deeply I adore you
(adoro te)

Plain Chant

Moderate tempo

Deep-ly I a-dore_ you, veiled di-vi-ni-ty

un-der-neath the signs I see you are tru-ly here

and to you I sur-ren-der, Love so strong, so near

con-tem-pla-ting you, my Love, leads to ec-sta-sy.

A - - - - men.

Thomas saw your hands and side: wounds I do not see
yet like him I call you Lord, call you God, adore
Jesus, let me believe in you ever more and more
Jesus, let me hope in you, love you utterly.

Sacrament of Calvary, Lover through and through
sacrament of Easter Day, gift of living Bread
let me savour your sweetness, purified and fed
giving thanks forevermore, drawing life from you.

Now I turn to you in faith: you are veiled from me
hidden Jesus, hear my prayer, give this longed-for grace
bring me out of the shadowlands, let me see your face
in your glory let me find joy eternally. Amen.

Come, Holy Ones
(Sancti, Venite)

Come, ho - ly ones share in His
Bo - dy come and re - ceive drink His re-
deem - ing Blood Eu - cha - rist - saved nour - ished in
sac - ra - ment come, let us sing our praise to God.

Body and Blood: sacrament setting free
we have been saved, rescued from Satan's pit
given for all, Saviour in sacrifice
he is the priest and he is gift.

Come nearer still, pure and with faith in him
let all receive gifts that will save and guard
First and the Last, Alpha and Omega
One who will come, the judge, the Lord.

Sancti, Venite (Come, Holy Ones) *is the best-known Eucharistic hymn of the early Irish Church. It comes from the* Antiphonary of Bangor *(now in the Ambrosian Library, Milan), compiled in the great monastery on the shore of Belfast Lough at the end of the seventh century.*

Greatest Sacrament
(Tantum Ergo)

Plain Chant

Moderate tempo

O come, a-dore this Sac-ra-ment, of sac-ra-ments the great-est this, Em-man-u-el so ve-ry near, ful-fill-ing all the pro-mi-ses. This ter-nal Three, e-ter-nal One. A-men.

This is the Bread the Father sent
the Lord in all reality
the senses open nothing here
it's faith alone that is the key

All glory to the Father sing
All glory to the Word, the Son
all glory to the Spirit bring
eternal Three, eternal One. Amen.

One Christ

Rather slowly

D   A7

For   all there is   one   Christ   for

D   A7   D7

all   one lov-ing   Lord is   sac-ri-ficed   one

G   A7   D

liv-ing Bread we   eat   to   bind and hold us

Em   D   Em A7 |1, 2 D

close and firm as   God's own bles-sed   wheat.   And

3 D   G   D

more.   A - - men.

And may this Eucharist-Gift
arise and shine across the world's dark drift
that all may see and come
and find in Him their All-Desired and in his love be one.

We praise You, Trinity
the Father, Son and Spirit, Blessed Three
we thank You and adore
and share in Eucharist the pledge of life forevermore.
Amen.

SOUL of CHRISt

Traditional English text slightly adapted

ne-ver let me be part-ed, Lord, from thee.

From the foe de - fend ____ me in death's hour

call _____ me bid me come

bid me to come to thee where I may praise thee,

Lord, e - ter - nal - ly.

CHRISTI SACRAMENTUM

African. Part of refrain by Saint Augustine

Moderate tempo

Chris - ti   sac - ra - men - tum

vin-clum ca-ri-ta-tis   ve-rum nu-tri-men-tum

sig-num u-ni-ta-tis   et mor-tis Do-mi-ni

Coda

De - o   gra - ti - as

Come and hear my teaching, I'm the Bread from heaven:
Panis pro amicis: I'm the Gift that's given to change you
through and through
Christi Sacramentum: vinclum caritatis:
verum nutrimentum: signum unitatis et mortis Domini

This is my commandment: love for one another:
meum est mandatum: you are sister, brother – so love as
I love you
Christi Sacramentum...

Don't forget my people: tell them I am living:
semper vivens ipsis: tell them I am giving: I'm their
redeemer too
Christi Sacramentum...

Bread for pilgrim journey: promise I will lead them:
Via in aeternum: into perfect freedom where everything
is new
Christi Sacramentum... Deo gratias

thank you for this Gift

African

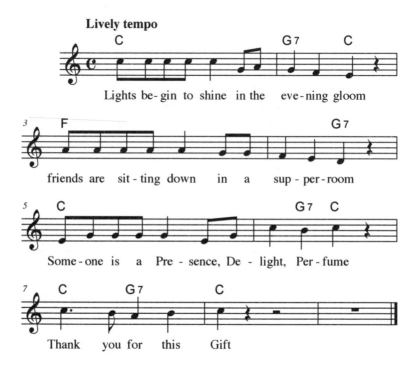

Lively tempo

Lights be- gin to shine in the eve-ning gloom

friends are sit - ting down in a sup - per - room

Some - one is a Pre - sence, De - light, Per - fume

Thank you for this Gift

They have been his friends from the very start
now the time has come for them all to part
love is coming now from his very Heart
thank you for this Gift.

Once he made a promise beside the sea
food and drink for living eternally
now the promise turns to reality
thank you for this Gift.

So there's something more than to talk and sup
bread is there before him, he takes it up
wine is there before him, he holds the cup
thank you for this Gift.

'This is all I am, take the living Bread
this is all I am, take the Blood that's shed
in this sign of death you'll have life instead'
thank you for this Gift.

'Do what I have done in my memory
pass it on to all who'll come after me
so I'll live in hearts that are yet to be'
thank you for this Gift.

Lord, we do believe in this simple sign
here beneath the shadows of bread and wine
you are truly present, you live and shine
thank you for this Gift.

Lord, you are our light in the days of gloom
come into our hearts, there is always room
Jesus, you are Presence, Delight, Perfume
thank you for this Gift.

O Sacramentum Pietatis

Refrain by Saint Augustine

O Sac-ra-men-tum pi - e - ta - tis,
sig - num nost - rae u - ni - ta - tis,
vin - cul - um - que ca - ri - ta - tis
Eu - cha - ris - ti - a

O come, receive enlightenment: let heart and face be radiant,
adoring, joyful, confident – receive the Eucharist
O Sacramentum pietatis, signum nostrae unitatis,
vinculumque caritatis – Eucharistia

O taste and see the Lord is good: He comes to be our daily food:
O mystery and gift of love – receive the Eucharist
O Sacramentum pietatis...

Around the altar let us stand and learn again his new command
to give to all our heart and hand and live the Eucharist
O Sacramentum pietatis...

CHRIST'S REALITY

Rather slowly

Here is our nour-ish-ment each day

Here is the Bread that comes from hea-ven

Here is the truth be-yond what we can see

Christ's re - al - i - ty.

Here is the joy to light our way
here is the cup of our refreshment
here is the truth to make us truly free
  —Christ's reality

A little bread, a little wine
these simple things of his creation
and they are changed by love so quietly
  —Christ's reality

The Lord so human and divine
the Son of Mary and the Father
so near to them, so near to you and me
  —Christ's reality

Here is the One who died and lives
here is the Lord of all his people
here is the bond of love and unity
  —Christ's reality

Here is the One who always gives
here is the promise of our glory
here is the sacrament of what we'll see
  —Christ's reality

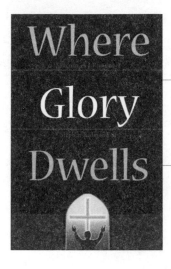

Where Glory Dwells

Stephen Redmond S.J.

Where Glory Dwells is a special type of autobiography, focusing on the author's experiences throughout his life of the atmosphere and mystery of churches and chapels.

All religious communities have their sanctuaries, their holy places: they serve a need of the human heart. Christian sanctuaries speak of God and life with God. They say in buildings and spaces what Saint Augustine said in words: 'You have made us for yourself, Lord, and our heart is restless until it rests in you… the Son of God, who is the father is the truth and the life, by taking our nature became the way'.

Ranging from faith to family life, from popular devotion to high art, *Where Glory Dwells* is a heart-warming and thought-provoking journey through sanctuaries both exalted and humble.

1 85390 673 5 • €7.95/£5.65

www.veritas.ie